AARON

AND

ALEXANDER

❧ Written and Illustrated by DON BROWN ❧

ROARING BROOK PRESS • NEW YORK

For my daughters, Sheahan and Corey,
borrowing Aaron Burr's words for his daughter, Theodosia:

*"I am indebted to you, my dearest … for a very great portion of the happiness which I have enjoyed
in this life. You have completely satisfied all that my heart and affections had hoped or wished."*

Copyright © 2015 by Don Brown
Published by Roaring Brook Press
Roaring Brook Press is a division of Holtzbrinck Publishing Holdings Limited Partnership
175 Fifth Avenue, New York, New York 10010
mackids.com

Library of Congress Cataloging-in-Publication Data

Brown, Don, 1949–
    Aaron and Alexander : the most famous duel in American history / Don Brown. — First edition.
        pages cm
    Audience: Ages 5–9.
    ISBN 978-1-59643-998-6 (hardcover)
    1. Burr-Hamilton Duel, Weehawken, N.J., 1804—Juvenile literature. 2. Hamilton, Alexander,
1757–1804—Juvenile literature. 3. Burr, Aaron, 1756–1836—Juvenile literature. I. Title.
    E302.6.H2B83 2015
    973.4092—dc23

                                                                                    2015003616

Roaring Brook Press books may be purchased for business or promotional use. For
information on bulk purchases please contact Macmillan Corporate and Premium Sales
Department at (800) 221-7945 x5442 or by email at specialmarkets@macmillan.com.

First edition 2015
Book design by Andrew Arnold
Printed in China by RR Donnelley Asia Printing Solutions Ltd., Dongguan City, Guangdong Province

1 3 5 7 9 10 8 6 4 2

AARON and ALEXANDER

could have been friends. They were alike in many ways.

But the ways in which they were different
made them the worst of enemies.

Aaron Burr was born amid the lush green fields and stately buildings of
Princeton college, New Jersey, surrounded by scholars and honored teachers.

Alexander Hamilton lived on the sun-drenched Caribbean island of St.
Croix with merchants, sailors, pirates, and plantation owners and their slaves.

In 1757, Aaron's father, a great educator, sickened and died. Within a year, his mother, grandfather, and grandmother also died from illness. Two-year-old Aaron and older sister Sally fell to their Uncle Timothy's care.

In 1768, a fever killed Alexander's mother, a shopkeeper. He and older brother James had been abandoned by their father years earlier and were now penniless and alone.

Both boys were orphans, but Aaron joined a large family that included young aunts and uncles, as well as Uncle Timothy's own children that eventually numbered fifteen.

Thirteen-year-old Alexander, on the other hand, was taken in by a generous merchant, while brother James went to live with a carpenter.

As a young boy, lively Aaron ran away from home . . . twice.
Once, he clambered aboard a ship with a mind to becoming a cabin
boy. Uncle Timothy retrieved him from the ship's mast.

Young Alexander saw ships not as a lark but as a livelihood.
He took work with a shipping company. Keen and serious, he even
ran the seaport business during his boss's
absence and made tough sea captains
jump to orders.

Aaron was smart. Uncle Timothy said he "learns bravely." Thirteen-year-old Aaron started at Princeton college in 1769.

Alexander was smart, too. After he survived a terrible hurricane, he wrote an attention-grabbing newspaper story about the storm. The story impressed island merchants who generously sent him to Columbia College to continue his education. Seventeen-year-old Alexander arrived in New York City and started school in 1772.

Aaron and Alexander grew into young men. Slender and small, each would bear "little" nicknames at times in their lives; for Aaron, Little Burr, and for Alexander, Little Lion.

Little Burr

Little Lion

Had it been another time, Aaron and Alexander might have devoted themselves to books and preparations for a life's work. But anger simmered among the American colonists against Great Britain. Their feelings of abuse by King George boiled over in 1776 and the American Revolution began. Aaron and Alexander staked their lives on independence.

The two small men showed great courage.
Daring Aaron joined an icy attack in Canada.
Brave Alexander dodged British cannonballs
in New York City.

They both fought the British in New York City. The English chased American troops out of the city and while Aaron and Alexander joined the retreat, their paths never crossed.

They both froze at the Army's winter camp in Valley Forge, Pennsylvania. Aaron threw his energies into commanding troops made unruly by the miserable, chilly camp. Alexander used his ambition to act as General George Washington's aide but still found time to read and study.
At war's end, Alexander took part in the great victory at the Battle of Yorktown. Aaron, however, was far from the action, worn out by army life.

The Revolution finally ended with the colonists' victory. Respected veterans of war, Aaron and Alexander became successful lawyers in New York City. They sometimes worked together, including successfully defending a man against sensational murder charges.

They shared meals. They shared friends.

"Good terms," said Alexander of his and Aaron's connection.

All the while, America wrote a constitution to govern itself. There would be no royalty and kings for the new republic. Alexander became the Constitution's greatest cheerleader. When George Washington became the first president, he made Alexander, his faithful aid from the war, the secretary of the treasury, making him responsible for the nation's money and finance.

Aaron was chosen as the United States senator from New York.

Americans everywhere wanted the young nation to be great, but deciding how to accomplish it made for angry disagreements. People took sides and political parties were born. Elections became heated, leaving the winners rejoicing and the losers stewing. Aaron and Alexander found themselves in opposing political camps.

Aaron enjoyed meeting people and pressing them for their vote, saying it made for "a great deal of fun."

Not for Alexander. To promote his own vision, the Little Lion wrote pamphlets and newspaper articles and earned a reputation for cutting insults of his political enemies. Hot-headed Alexander described second President John Adam as vain, jealous, and unstable.

Alexander said Aaron was a man of "extreme and irregular ambition . . . more cunning than wise," who lacked "solid abilities" and surrounded himself with the "worst people."

Aaron mostly ignored the attacks that continued on and off for years.

Then in 1800 Aaron ran for president of the United States against Thomas Jefferson, who was expected to win. It was a fierce campaign, each side being sure of its absolute rightness and the other side's outright wickedness. When the results came in. Aaron had tied the election! The House of Representatives held a special runoff vote.

The thought of Aaron as president distressed Alexander.

"Cunning . . . wicked . . . one of the worst men," Alexander said of Aaron. "Burr loves nothing but himself . . . The appointment of Burr as president would disgrace our country abroad."

Alexander helped build opposition against Aaron. After thirty-six ballots, Jefferson won the presidency and Aaron settled for vice president.

In spite of his high office, Aaron discovered he had little power or influence. In 1804 he decided to run for governor of New York State . . . and lost.

Alexander had opposed him again.

"Despicable," Alexander had said of Aaron.

It was a small word, but an awful one, and it struck Aaron hard.

"It became impossible that I could . . . with self respect forbear," he said, meaning he could not longer brush off Alexander's attacks.

Aaron demanded an apology but none came.

So Aaron challenged Alexander to a duel.

Dueling—fighting with swords or pistols to settle an argument, especially those involving "honor" or reputation—wasn't unusual. Before becoming president, Andrew Jackson killed a man in a duel. Prior to his presidency, James Monroe challenged none other than Alexander Hamilton to a duel! It was settled before gunplay—in fact, Alexander settled eleven duels peacefully before Aaron challenged him. Aaron had fought one duel; the opponent's bullet pierced his coat but not his body.

Alexander accepted Aaron's challenge.

Just days before their duel, Aaron and Alexander attended the same party for veterans of the Revolution as if their deadly argument had never happened. Alexander even climbed onto a table and sang a song.

At dawn on July 11, 1804, Aaron and Alexander separately rode small boats across the Hudson River from New York City to Weehawken, New Jersey. With each man was a "second," a friend to help with the duel.

At sunrise, a distance of thirty feet was marked off. At the seconds' command, Aaron and Alexander—the two orphans, the two patriots, the two war veterans, the two public servants of the new nation—took their places, raised pistols, aimed, and . . .

Alexander's shot missed.

Aaron's did not.

The wounded Alexander was carried home where he died the following day.

New York City held a great funeral for Alexander Hamilton, hero of the Revolution and champion of the Constitution.

Much of the country cursed Aaron Burr. He never recovered his political reputation. He wandered Europe for several years. When he was an old man, a thoughtful Aaron said, "I should have known the world was wide enough for Hamilton and me."

AUTHOR'S NOTE

AARON BURR *and* **ALEXANDER HAMILTON:** It is almost impossible to peer through the lens of history and not see the two conjoined. Whatever their individual achievements or failures, a discussion of one inevitably includes the other.

The year of Alexander's birth on Nevis is uncertain; scholars argue whether it was 1755 or 1757. His mother, Rachel Faucette, had two bad marriages, but tried to make the best of them. She hadn't acquired a divorce from her first husband when she took up with James Hamilton and had two sons, one of whom was Alexander. Some evidence suggests Alexander's real father was the rich merchant Thomas Stevens, helping explain why orphan Alexander was taken in by Stevens and the extraordinary resemblance Alexander bore to Stevens's legitimate son.

Aaron Burr entered life with unimaginable grief when his immediate family died from disease. Fortunately, Aaron had a thoughtful guardian in his uncle, Timothy Edward, who was determined to make young Aaron an educated gentleman and had the financial means to achieve it.

Both men were smart and well-read. Both were brave and proved their mettle on Revolutionary War battlefields. Each acted as wartime aides for George Washington, Aaron forsaking the job almost immediately in response to his dislike for Washington, while Alexander held on for several years before the general's prickliness drove him away.

The emergence of the new American republic and the concurrent rise of political parties put Alexander and Aaron at odds. Burr found himself the target of stiff political attacks—many times at the hands of Hamilton and his allies—and the damage to his reputation was considerable. But the truthfulness of the attacks is debatable, inflaming the passions of scholars to this day.

Less debatable is their comparable impact on America. Hamilton sat with the committee that wrote the Constitution, championed the document by authoring most of the Federalist Papers, and insured the financial backbone of country by his actions as the first secretary of treasury. Burr was an inconsequential senator and vice president.

The arcane political infighting of the 1800 election nearly awarded Burr the presidency. In the end, however, Thomas Jefferson won. Burr later lost a bid to be New York's governor, climaxing with Burr challenging Hamilton in a duel for his comments during the campaign. Dueling was illegal in both New York and New Jersey but enforcement of the law was spotty. Growing public disfavor of the practice would eventually push it from the American scene by the Civil War.

Aaron and Alexander met in the woods with pistols, and Alexander was killed. Questions about who fired first, and whether Hamilton, ostensibly the greater gentleman, fired in the air rather than at his opponent, still carom through the halls of history. But testimony supporting one man over the other is thin, and the truth is forever lost to time. Still, Burr's supposed villainy in the duel has found its way into conventional wisdom.

Despite his tarnished reputation, I find myself in Burr's corner. His flaws appear to me less as failings and more as unsubstantiated bad press. And I'm drawn to his apparent humanity and genuineness, especially in regard to his devotion to his beloved wife and daughter.

Burr and Hamilton were ensnared by the cultural conventions of their day; the death of one was ostensibly needed to satisfy the honor of the other. In the end, nothing was accomplished but tragedy.

BIBLIOGRAPHY

Brands, H. W. *The Heartbreak of Aaron Burr.* New York: Anchor Books, 2012.

Brookhiser, Richard. *Alexander Hamilton, American.* New York: Touchstone, 2000.

Chernow, Ron. *Alexander Hamilton.* New York: Penguin Books, 2005.

Isenberg, Nancy. *Fallen Founder: The Life of Aaron Burr.* New York: Penguin Books, 2008.

Kennedy, Roger G. *Burr, Hamilton, and Jefferson: A Study in Character.* New York: Oxford University Press, 2000.

PBS. *The American Experience: The Duel.* pbs.org/wgbh/amex/duel/filmmore/transcript/transcript1.html

Rogow, Arnold A. *A Fatal Friendship: Alexander Hamilton and Aaron Burr.* New York: Hill & Wang, 1998.

St. George, Judith. *The Duel: The Parallel Lives of Alexander Hamilton and Aaron Burr.* New York: Viking, 2009.